PATHFINDERS
IN EXPLORATION

Exploring the Oceans

SCHOOLHOUSE PRESS

Copyright © 1988 by Schoolhouse Press, Inc.
160 Gould Street, Needham
Massachusetts 02194
ISBN 0-8086-1163-1 (hardback)
ISBN 0-8086-1170-4 (paperback)

Original copyright, © Macmillan Education Limited 1987

Authors: Derek Cullen and John Murray-Robertson

Editorial planning: AMR

Designed and typeset by The Pen and Ink Book Company Ltd, London

Illustrated by Gecko Ltd

Picture research by Faith Perkins

Printed in Hong Kong

88/89/90/91/92/93   6 5 4 3 2 1

Photographic Credits

t=top b=bottom l=left r=right

The author and publishers wish to acknowledge, with thanks, the following photographic sources: 20*r* J Allan Cash, London; 10, 22-23, 24 Barnaby's Picture Library, London; contents (Weidenfeld Archive), 14*l*, 19*b*, 25, 26*b* BBC Hulton Picture Library, London; 14*r*, 16, 30-31 Mary Evans Picture Library, London; 4, 6, 7*b*, 8*r*, 18, 26*t*, 33*b* (Collection Mrs Rienits) Michael Holford; 36 Knudsen information as, Oslo; title, 35*b* Kon-Tiki Museet, Oslo; 5*l* and *r*, 28, 29, 33*t*, 38 National Maritime Museum, London photographs Michael Holford; 7*t*, 8*l*, 9, 11*t* and *b*, 12, 13*t*, 17, 19*t*, 20*l*, 22*l*, 23*b*, 27, 28*l* Peter Newark's Historical Pictures; 41, 42, 43 Pickthall Picture Library; 30*l*, 31*b* Picturepoint (UK); 39*b* Planet Earth Pictures; 37*l* and *r*, 40 Popperfoto, London; 39*t* US Navy/MARS, UK; contents, 13*b* (Foto MAS), 19*b* Weidenfeld Archive

Cover photograph courtesy of Kon Tiki Museet, Oslo.

The publishers have made every effort to trace the copyright holders, but if they have inadvertently overlooked any, they will be pleased to make the necessary arrangement at the first opportunity.

Note to the reader
In this book there are some words in the text which are printed in **bold** type. This shows that the word is listed in the glossary on page 46. The glossary gives a brief explanation of words which may be new to you.

Contents

Introduction

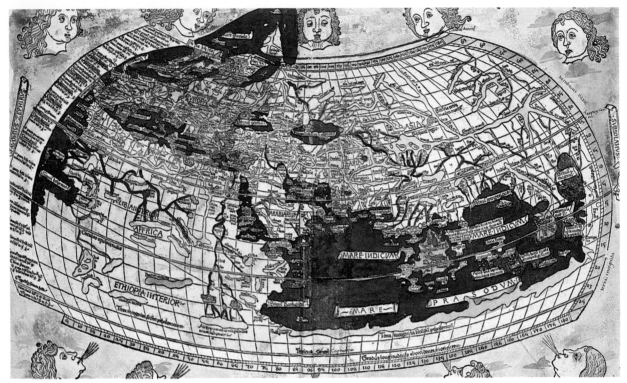

▲ This map was made in 1486. The coasts of Europe and Arabia have the most detail. This was because trade had been carried out between people living on the shores of the Mediterranean Sea, the Atlantic Ocean, and the Indian Ocean for several hundred years. People knew very little about the southern or western parts of the world at that time.

The oceans cover almost three quarters of the surface of the world. The Pacific Ocean alone is greater in area than all the **continents**. There are five oceans: the Arctic, the Antarctic, the Atlantic, the Indian, and the Pacific Oceans. Large areas of the Arctic Ocean and the Antarctic Ocean are frozen. In this book, you will find out about the people who have made great sea journeys, or **voyages**, on these oceans.

How the Oceans Were Explored

The oceans are not easy to cross. In the past, sailors had very few instruments to help them to **navigate**. They could only figure out where their ship was by knowing their speed and by looking at the sky. This is how they set their **course**. They used the position of the sun and the stars. The first sailors had to learn how to build ships that were strong enough to survive storms and high waves. Some of these ships were rowed by teams of oarsmen. Other ships used the wind which filled their sails and carried them over the water. Slowly, sails took over from oars. The ships became faster and easier to handle.

▲ The compass is one of the oldest aids to navigation. It was invented by the Chinese. It has a magnetic needle that always points north. This compass dates from 1750.

▲ This instrument is called a sextant. Sextants are used to measure the angle between the sun or a star and the horizon. They help navigators to figure out their positions.

The sailors' health was a real problem. On long journeys, the ships were often out of sight of the land. The seamen became sick if the ship did not carry enough drinking water, food, and fruit. Ships had to be very large in order for them to carry enough supplies for long voyages. Also, they had to be **stable**, so that they would not turn over in rough seas.

Why Explore the Oceans?

The first long ocean journeys started in the Mediterranean Sea. From there, the explorers went into the Atlantic Ocean and around Africa into the Indian Ocean. Later, there were journeys which started out from the north of Europe to cross the Atlantic. The early explorers went on voyages for many reasons. Many were **traders** who went to find silk and spices in Asia, or the **East**, as it was called.

Others wanted to map, or **chart**, the seas. Also, there were explorers who wanted to find new lands. They hoped that these lands would contain gold and spices which they could bring back to their countries.

What Makes an Ocean Explorer?

The explorers in this book were all expert sailors before they set out. Many of them felt more at home on a ship than on land. They were ready to take great risks, and often to go where no one had been before. Often, they forced their **crews** to sail into unknown areas when the crews were really afraid to sail on any farther. The famous ocean explorer, Captain James Cook, said that he wanted to go "not only farther than anyone had been before, but as far as it was possible for man to go."

5

Early Ocean Explorers

The first peoples who lived along the edge of the Mediterranean Sea learned to sail from place to place by keeping close to the **coast**. A few thousand years ago, Egypt was a rich and powerful country. The people who lived there built boats which sailed up and down the Nile River. These boats were not sturdy enough for the sea. The real sailors of the Mediterranean were the Phoenicians.

The Phoenicians lived in a part of the Middle East which we call Lebanon today. They were rich traders. They built cities around the Mediterranean Sea. From these cities, they set out on longer and longer voyages. These people were looking for silver and tin. They sailed out into the Atlantic Ocean in search of these **metals**. Their strong boats had flat bottoms and large storage places, or **holds**. This was where their trade goods, or **cargo**, were stored. We know that these people got as far north as Ireland and the south of Britain.

There is one voyage we know a lot about. This was the voyage of Hanno of Carthage. Over 2,400 years ago, Hanno took sixty-seven ships with him. Each of these ships had fifty oars. He sailed from Carthage on the North African coast. He sailed through the Strait of Gibraltar and into the Atlantic Ocean. Hanno's aim was to set up new trading cities down the west coast of Africa. His voyage took him as far as Sierra Leone. Then, he was forced to return because his men did not have enough food.

Pytheas the Greek

Over 2,000 years ago, a Greek named Pytheas set sail in search of tin. He made the longest journey we know of at that time. He sailed up the coasts of Spain and France. Then, Pytheas crossed the English Channel and found the tin mines of southern Britain. From there, he went up the east coast of Britain and Scotland. Then, he sailed across the open sea to a country he called Thule. We think this was Norway or Iceland because his story mentions frozen seas.

◀ The Phoenicians traded throughout the Mediterranean Sea about 3,000 years ago. This carving on stone shows one of their ships that is being rowed by a team of oarsmen.

▶ The Greeks sailed all around the Mediterranean Sea, and along the coast of northern Europe. The bigger ship on the left could probably carry about 100 tons of cargo in its hold.

The Viking Explorers

About 1,100 years ago, the people of Scandinavia started to make many long voyages. These people were called the Vikings. They were looking for new lands to live in. They rowed their longboats through the rough northern seas. We know these fearless sailors crossed the North Sea to Iceland and Greenland where many of them settled.

In the year 1,000, Lief Ericcson sailed from Greenland with many longboats, to the coast of North America. He and his men spent the winter in Newfoundland before going back to Greenland. A few more ships crossed the open sea to Newfoundland, but most of the Vikings still kept close to their own coasts.

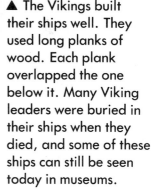

▲ The Vikings built their ships well. They used long planks of wood. Each plank overlapped the one below it. Many Viking leaders were buried in their ships when they died, and some of these ships can still be seen today in museums.

Gateway to Asia

Over 1,000 years ago, goods like silk, jewels, fine carpets, and spices came from Asia only. They had to be carried across overland **routes** to Europe. Then, the Mongols took over most of Asia in the early 1200's. Their ruler, Kublai Khan, let **merchants** set up overland routes to China. The most famous of these merchant explorers was Marco Polo. In 1271, he set out from Venice with his father and uncle to China. It took them three and a half years to cross the mountains and deserts.

▲ In the 1200's, Marco Polo traveled from Italy to Asia. When he returned home, he wrote a book about his travels. Many people refused to believe his stories.

When the Polos reached China, Kublai Khan made them welcome. Marco spent sixteen years traveling around Southeast Asia. He even visited the spice island of Java. The Polos returned to Venice in 1295. They brought back jewels and fine silk robes from China.

A Sea Route to Asia

Many merchants used the land route to China after the Polos' journey. Then, in the 1400's, the Turks began to gain power in the eastern Mediterranean. These people were hostile to Europe because of a religious conflict. In 1453, they took control of Constantinople. This was the main trading city on the route between Asia and Europe. This closed the land route to the East for the merchants. Now, the only way appeared to be to sail south, then east. Sailors at that time, however, were afraid of going south. They thought this route led to the hot, or fiery, center of the world.

◀ Bartolomeu Dias led the first ships from Europe to sail right around the Cape of Good Hope at the tip of Africa. It was so stormy that they did not see it the first time they passed it. Dias was shipwrecked and drowned off this Cape, in 1500.

Prince Henry the Navigator

One man helped sailors to overcome their fear of sailing south. He was born in Portugal in 1394. His name was Henry, and he was King John of Portugal's second son. He became known as Prince Henry the Navigator.

Prince Henry wanted to find a new route to Asia. He was also a Christian, and wanted to spread the message of Christ. In 1418, Henry started a school of navigation. There, the sailors would learn all that was known about the oceans. Also, at this time, the Portuguese built a new, faster, and safer ship called a **caravel**. From about 1420, Prince Henry began to send captains in these caravels to explore the west coast of Africa.

◀ From 1420, Prince Henry the Navigator paid sailors to make several journeys down the west coast of Africa. He never made any of these journeys himself. However, without his efforts the discovery of a route to India might have been made much later.

However, the captains and their sailors were afraid of the fiery area, or **region**, which they thought was farther south. The ships did not go any farther than Cape Bojador. At last, in 1433, the sailors overcame their fear and ships went beyond the Cape. Year by year, ships went farther down the coast. In 1486, Captain Cão got to Cape Cross on the shore of the Namib Desert. He had to turn back because he did not have enough drinking water on board.

The next year, Captain Bartolomeu Dias took two caravels and a supply ship on a voyage down the African coast. When he had sailed even farther than Cão, a storm blew him away from the coast. When the storm was over, the sailors sailed eastward looking for land. When they found none, they realized that they had rounded the tip of Africa called the Cape of Good Hope. Dias had found the way to the Indian Ocean. Other people followed, but the route took too long. People thought there must be a better way to get to Asia.

What If the World Is Round?

▲ Christopher Columbus was born in Genoa, Italy in 1451. He first went to sea when he was fourteen. He sailed across the Atlantic Ocean four times. He set up Spain's first colonies in the Caribbean.

About 500 years ago, many people believed that the world was flat. But people who had read books on navigation thought that the world was round. One of these people was Christopher Columbus.

Columbus was an Italian, but he was employed as a sailor by Portugal. He wanted to find a new route to Asia and the Spice Islands of the East. Today, we know these as the Moluccas in Indonesia. Columbus had an idea which was new for his time. He believed he could reach the East by going west around the world across the Atlantic Ocean. He had heard stories of pieces of carved wood found drifting off the coast of Madeira and the Canary Islands. These pieces of wood appeared to have floated across the oceans from the west. Also, he heard of the body of a man that was washed up on these beaches. This body did not look like a person from Europe or Africa. He felt sure that he would find land if he sailed west.

Columbus Looks for Support

A number of scientists and explorers had tried to figure out how much of the world was covered by land. Columbus read their books and came to believe that only one seventh of the world was covered by sea. He estimated from this that it was about 3,750 miles across the Atlantic Ocean to Asia. He had no idea of where he would land.

◀ Columbus saying "goodbye" to the King and Queen of Spain. Few people believed that he would reach Asia by sailing west. They thought that Columbus would never return from the journey.

▼ Columbus set off in 1492 with three wooden sailing ships. The *Santa Maria*, pictured here was a carrack. The *Niña* and the *Pinta* were both caravels. Caravels were smaller than carracks, and they were often used by ocean explorers in the 1400's.

Columbus needed to find someone who would pay for the journey, or **expedition**. At last, in 1484, King Ferdinand and Queen Isabella of Spain agreed to pay for the voyage. They hoped that Columbus would make Spain rich by finding gold and spices and a new trading route to Asia.

The Voyage West Begins

On August 3, 1492, Columbus set sail from Palos in Spain. He sailed with three small ships. Columbus's ship, the *Santa Maria* was 114 feet long and had a crew of fifty men. The other two ships, the *Niña* and the *Pinta*, were smaller. The *Niña* carried a crew of thirty, and the *Pinta* carried a crew of twenty-four. The ships were captained by two brothers, Martín and Vicente Pinzón. Few of the crew knew much about sailing. Many of them had only gone along to make their fortunes. Others were **convicts**. They had been let out of prison for the voyage.

The voyage did not start well. The *Pinta* broke her steering wheel, or **helm**, when they were only three days out from Spain. After they had repaired the *Pinta*, the three ships left the Canary Islands on September 6. Then, some Portuguese ships tried to stop them. The Portuguese did not want anyone to find a new route to Asia. Columbus was able to escape, and he set off into the unknown.

Crossing the Atlantic

The crew became afraid when they had been at sea for over two weeks. They began to doubt that they would ever see land again. Columbus knew that they had sailed a long way, but he did not want the crew to know this. He kept notes of the voyage. These are called **logbooks**. In one logbook, he wrote the real distances. In the other, he put shorter distances for the crew to see.

As they sailed on, some of the men became sick with **scurvy**. This may have been because they did not have the right food. They had salted meat and dried biscuits, but no fresh fruit or vegetables. After about two weeks on the open sea, many of the crew wanted to turn back. Columbus talked to his men and persuaded them to keep going.

The First Sight of Land

A few days after this, the ships reached an area thick with seaweed called the Sargossa Sea. Columbus tried to keep his men's spirits up. He told them that the seaweed was a sign of land nearby. Then, they saw flocks of birds over the ships. The other two captains said this must mean land was close. On September 25, Martin Pinzón shouted out that he could see land ahead. All the men thought they could see land, too, but it was a trick of the light. After this, the crews were very unhappy. Some of the men wanted to turn against Columbus and **mutiny**. Columbus said he would not punish the people who wanted to mutiny if they would just wait for a few more days. The ships changed course to the southwest. On the evening of October 11, Columbus saw the faint light of a fire ahead. They had sighted land at last!

▼ Columbus's sailors were afraid they would never reach the end of their journey. They were also afraid they would never get home.

The West Indies

The next day, Columbus, the two captains, and a large group of men went ashore on an island. This island is now called Watling Island, and is part of the Bahamas. Columbus, however, was sure he had found the Spice Islands. He called the island San Salvador. For the next few days, Columbus and his men traveled to other islands nearby.

Columbus called the people of the islands Indians because he thought that he had found a part of Asia called the Indies. The island people were friendly to Columbus and his crew. They told Columbus of a larger island with gold. Although he had found some spices, Columbus had not found gold. Gold was what the Spanish wanted.

▲ Columbus and his crew, about to land on the island of San Salvador in 1492. They thought they had reached Asia.

▼ This map was drawn in 1500. It was the first map to show the "new world" of America. Columbus had reached it first in 1492.

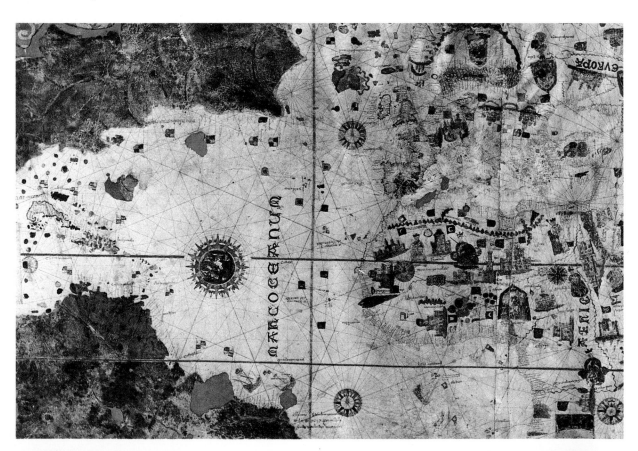

Columbus and the Indies

The island that the Indians had spoken of was Cuba. Columbus believed it was Japan, and set sail at once. The ships reached Cuba on October 28, 1492. The people there were shy, but friendly. They told Columbus that there was gold inland and precious jewels, called **pearls**, in the sea. Columbus was sure he had found Japan, and thought China could not be far away. Martin Pinzón may have thought this, too. In any case, he slipped off in secret with his ship, the *Pinta*.

Columbus left Cuba in early December, and sailed to Haiti. He called the island Hispaniola. There, he found plenty of gold, and the local people were ready to give him some in exchange for small gifts.

▲ The harbor and city of Havana on the island of Cuba. When Columbus landed in Cuba, he claimed the island for Spain. This picture was drawn in the 1800's, about 300 years after Columbus first saw the island.

On December 5, the *Santa María* was anchored off the north of Haiti. The sea was calm. All appeared to be well. There was only a young boy in charge of the ship. Somehow, the ship ran aground onto the rocks. There was no way the men could get her off.

Now, Columbus had only one small ship left, the *Niña*. Therefore, he did what appeared to be the best thing to do. He left thirty-nine men with weapons and supplies on the island, and he set sail for Spain. These men were never seen again.

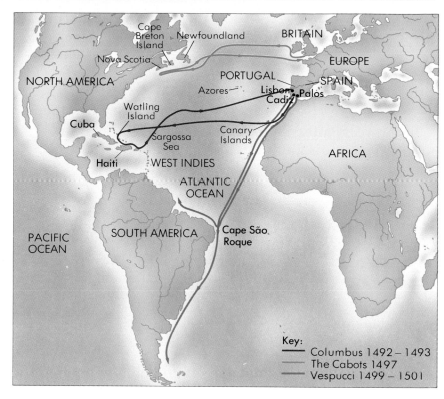

◀ At first, the Caribbean people were very friendly to Columbus. They gave him gifts of gold. Later, the Spanish took huge amounts of gold from South America by force.

▶ The voyages of Christopher Columbus, John and Sebastian Cabot, and Amerigo Vespucci across the Atlantic Ocean.

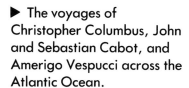

The Return Voyage

After Columbus had been at sea for two days, he met up with the *Pinta* and its captain, Martin Pinzón. Pinzón told him his men had taken over the *Pinta*, and had sailed it away from Haiti. Columbus was angry, but the two ships set the same course for Spain. Columbus was afraid that they would not get back safely. He dropped a barrel over the side of the ship. In the barrel, he put a message telling of their discovery.

The voyage home was stormy, and the men feared that they would sink. At last, they sighted the islands to the west of Portugal called the Azores. They knew the worst was over. They anchored off the island of Santa Maria, and went ashore. The governor of the island did not welcome the Spanish ships and

seamen. Even though the weather was stormy, Columbus thought that it would be best to set sail for Spain. The *Niña* and the *Pinta* lost each other in a fierce storm. They did not find each other again until they reached Spain.

On March 15, 1493, Columbus reached Spain. He was welcomed by the King and Queen. They were very pleased with his discoveries.

The Importance of Columbus

Columbus made three more voyages across the Atlantic Ocean. On one of these voyages, he saw the mainland of America. Columbus did not know that he had found a new continent, but after his voyage, many people followed his route across the Atlantic Ocean.

New Routes to Asia

In the years after Columbus's voyages, more and more sailors wanted to find a route to Asia. The Portuguese wanted to get back the sea power they had had under Prince Henry the Navigator. Captain Dias had found a way around Africa. Columbus had found the coast of America. Now, people wanted to explore further.

A Route to India

In July, 1497, the Portuguese set out on another voyage. Their aim was to find a sea route to India by going around the Cape of Good Hope. They wanted to trade in spices with the local rulers in India.

The leader of the expedition was Vasco da Gama. He took four ships, and followed Captain Dias's route down the west coast of Africa. After ninety-six days at sea, many of the crew got scurvy. On November 4, da Gama put in at St. Helena Bay in order to find fresh food and water. Then, he set off to sail around the Cape. The voyage was stormy. As they entered the Indian Ocean, the strong flow, or **current**, of the ocean made their progress very slow.

Da Gama sailed north up the east coast of Africa. Da Gama wanted to find a **pilot** to guide his ships to India. At the port of Malindi, a local ruler found a pilot for da Gama. The pilot guided da Gama's ships across the Indian Ocean. They reached the Indian trading port of Calicut on May 18, 1498.

After three months in India, da Gama and his ships set off again across the Indian Ocean to Malindi. It was a long voyage because the strong **monsoon** winds were blowing against them. After sailing around the Cape of Good Hope, they reached Portugal at last in September, 1499.

▶ The King of Portugal with Vasco da Gama before he set sail from Portugal in 1497. He was the first person from Europe to sail right around Africa, and across the Indian Ocean.

▲ John and Sebastian Cabot, just before they sailed from Bristol in the west of England. John Cabot went to North America twice. The second time, he was shipwrecked and drowned.

The Coast of South America

In 1499, an Italian merchant named Amerigo Vespucci sailed from Cádiz in Spain. Like Columbus, he wanted to reach Asia by sailing west across the Atlantic Ocean. Vespucci reached the northeastern point of South America called Cape São Roque in Brazil. From there, he sailed northwest along the coast of South America. He saw the mouth of a large river which today we know as the Amazon.

In 1501, Vespucci made another voyage. He sailed from Lisbon in Portugal to Cape São Roque again, and then down the coast of South America. Amerigo knew that he had not found Asia, but a "new world." He had sailed along almost all of the east coast of South America. Later, the continent was called America after his first name, Amerigo.

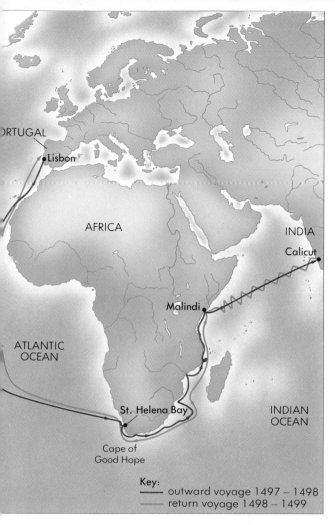

▲ Vasco da Gama's voyage to India.

The Coast of North America

In 1497, John Cabot and his son, Sebastian, set sail from England. They were searching for a western route to Asia. Their route took them across the Atlantic to Cape Breton Island near Nova Scotia, and then on to Newfoundland. They thought that they had found Asia, but they saw no people living there. On a second voyage in 1498, John Cabot sailed south down the east coast of North America as far as Delaware Bay.

17

Around the World

After Vasco da Gama's voyage to India, Portugal led the control of the trade routes in the Indian Ocean. Other countries wanted to trade with India too, but they had to find another route.

A Portuguese sea captain named Ferdinand Magellan thought he knew of a new route to India and the Spice Islands. When the King of Portugal was not interested in Magellan's new route, he went to the King of Spain. King Charles V of Spain agreed to help him.

Magellan's Plan

Magellan had spent a lot of time in Portugal looking at the latest maps. He had also talked to Rui Faleiro, a famous mapmaker. Faleiro thought it would be possible to get through from the Atlantic to the Pacific Ocean. He thought this could be done by going through a narrow channel, or **strait**, in the southern part of America. Magellan planned to sail around the world, and King Charles agreed to pay for the expedition.

▼ This map was made in the 1500's. It shows two ships about to enter the Strait of Magellan. This was the route Magellan took around the tip of South America.

The Expedition Begins

Charles V gave Magellan five ships. They were old and required a lot of repairs to make them sturdy enough for the long journey that was planned. Magellan loaded the ships with food. He took on salted beef, fish, cheese, oil, and dried beans and peas. On board, there were also rifles, or **muskets**, and bullets. Also, the crew carried goods to trade for spices. On September 20, 1519, Magellan set sail. He did not tell the crews what they were trying to do. He was afraid they would refuse to sail with him.

Across the South Atlantic

Many of the men asked where they were going, but Magellan refused to tell them. They sailed on across the Atlantic Ocean, and reached Rio de Janeiro in December. There, they traded beads and mirrors for food. After that, they sailed down to the River Plate. Magellan thought that the river was the way through to the Pacific Ocean. As they sailed up the river, it grew narrower and the ships had to turn back.

▲ Magellan spent a year getting ready for his voyage around the world. He took 237 sailors with him in five ships. One of these ships, the *San Antonio*, turned around and sailed back to Spain when it reached the Strait of Magellan.

Magellan spent the winter in a large **bay** farther south called Port San Julián. The weather was very cold, and little grew on the land. There was no way of getting fresh supplies of food. It was too cold to go on, and Magellan refused to turn back.

In June, 1520, Magellan was ready to set sail again. The men were hungry and angry. Some of them planned a mutiny. Magellan heard of the plan, and he had the leaders put to death. After this, the men agreed to obey Magellan.

◄ Magellan made a special study of astronomy and navigation. These are some of the navigation instruments that he used on his journey around the world.

Through the Strait

Magellan sent one of his ships, the *Santiago*, to explore the coast farther south. He hoped to find a strait leading from the Atlantic Ocean to the Pacific Ocean. The *Santiago* failed to find the strait, and was **wrecked**. Only one man was saved.

In October, Magellan sent the *Concepción* and the *San Antonio* to look for the strait. After two days, they came back with the news that they had found a route. Magellan sailed on into the strait with the four ships he had left. One of these, the *San Antonio*, slipped away and went back to Spain. The ship carried a lot of Magellan's supplies.

▲ Magellan and some of the sailors, just before they entered the Strait of Magellan. It was a very dangerous journey through the Strait. Often, Magellan went ahead of his ships in a small boat to find the best route.

The voyage through the strait took thirty-eight days, even though the distance is only 350 miles. The route ahead was hard to follow because it twisted and turned between small islands. They named the strait the Strait of Magellan. As the ships sailed into the Pacific Ocean, Magellan wept with joy.

Ocean of Death

Magellan now knew he could sail northwest and reach the Spice Islands. What Magellan did not know was how far he had to go. The ships were at sea two months without any sight of land. They had started off with little food, and now they had none. The men even ate the leather straps from the ships' **masts** and the rats aboard the ships. All the men had scurvy.

▲ Magellan's own cross is inside this cross on the island of Cebu, in the Philippines. Magellan taught the leaders of Cebu to be Christians.

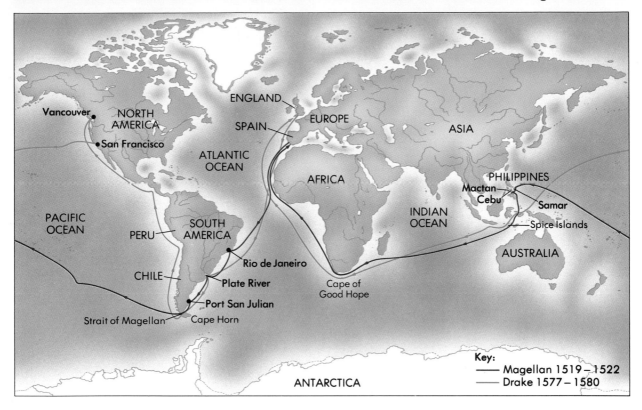

The Death of Magellan

In early March, 1521, the ships discovered the Philippines. There, the crew were given two weeks' rest. Then, they sailed around the islands. They were going to trade for spices and tell the people about Christianity.

About a month later, they landed at an island called Cebu. There, the ruler of the island asked Magellan to help him fight some of his enemies on the nearby island of Mactan. Magellan took a group of his men with him. They were armed with muskets. They landed on Mactan and called to the islanders to come and talk, but the islanders wanted to fight. There was a fierce battle. Magellan and forty of his men were killed.

▲ The voyages of Ferdinand Magellan and Sir Francis Drake around the world.

The men who were left had to burn the *Concepcíon* because there were not enough sailors to sail the ship. There were only 115 men left out of the 237 who had sailed from Spain. The *Vittoria* and the *Trinidad* sailed on to the Spice Islands. They reached these islands in November, 1521.

The men bought spices in the islands. Then, they sailed for Spain across the Indian Ocean and around the Cape of Good Hope. In September, 1522, only the *Vittoria* reached Spain with eighteen men. They were the first people to sail around the world.

The English Pirate

The next man to sail around the world was Sir Francis Drake, an English seaman and trader. He had a reputation as a pirate, too. He wanted to sail into the Pacific Ocean to attack Spanish ships along the coasts of Chile and Peru. These ships carried silver. Also, Drake hoped to find another continent south of America.

▲ Francis Drake was born in Devon, England in 1540. After his successful voyage around the world, he was knighted by Queen Elizabeth 1. He became Sir Francis Drake.

The *Golden Hind*

In December, 1577, Drake left England with three ships. His own ship was called the *Pelican*. During the voyage, he changed the name to the *Golden Hind*. The other ships were the *Elizabeth* and the *Marigold*.

Before the ships set sail, Drake told the crews that they were sailing to Alexandria in Egypt. He knew that they would be afraid to go through the Strait of Magellan. They were angry when he told them the truth. Some of the men tried to mutiny when they reached Port San Julián on the coast of South America. This was the place where Magellan's men had tried to mutiny also. Drake, like Magellan, had to put the leader of the mutiny to death.

▲ This is a replica of Drake's ship, the *Golden Hind*. It is really very small when compared with the ocean-going ships of today.

In August, 1578, Drake and his three ships entered the Strait of Magellan. It took them seventeen days to reach the Pacific Ocean. There, they ran into very bad storms which went on for fifty-two days. The *Marigold* sank, and all its crew were drowned. The captain of the *Elizabeth* decided to sail back through the Strait, and return to England.

Drake's ship, the *Golden Hind*, was blown far to the south of Cape Horn. This is at the southern tip of South America. At last, the storm ended, and Drake was able to set a course up the coast of Chile and Peru. He took the Spanish by surprise, and filled his ship with silver and other treasures.

▲ Drake was often called a pirate because he attacked Spanish ships, and took the gold they carried back to Spain from South America.

Crossing the Pacific

Drake did not plan to return through the Strait of Magellan. He thought there was another sea route from the Pacific Ocean to the Atlantic Ocean farther north. He sailed north past Vancouver, which was farther north than anyone had been before him. He could not find the sea route he was looking for, so he turned back. From there, he sailed down to San Francisco. From San Francisco, Drake sailed across the Pacific Ocean to the Spice Islands. The *Golden Hind* ran onto rocks there, and Drake almost lost his ship. He put into port, and loaded a cargo of spices on the ship.

The *Golden Hind* sailed back to England across the Indian Ocean and around the Cape of Good Hope. Drake's voyage had taken almost three years.

The Northwest Passage

Many sailors thought that there must be a route to Asia around the north of America. The Cabots had explored the east coast of Canada. Drake had sailed up the west coast. These men did not find the route they were looking for.

In 1576, an English seaman named Martin Frobisher sailed into the icy Arctic Ocean. He went as far as Baffin Island where he thought that he had found a strait which might lead to the Pacific Ocean. It was too full of ice to sail through. Other famous seamen tried to find this Northwest Passage. One of them, Sir Humphrey Gilbert, died at sea. Another, John Davis, was driven back by the ice and fog.

▲ Sir Humphrey Gilbert set out from Plymouth, England in June, 1583. He reached Newfoundland in August. Then, he took his ship farther south, but he was shipwrecked and drowned.

Hudson and the Fur Trade

In 1609, an English seaman named Henry Hudson set out to find the Northwest Passage. He was working for the Dutch. The Dutch East India Company wanted to find a shorter trading route to Asia. The route around Africa was too long and dangerous.

▲ The route of Henry Hudson in search of the Northwest Passage.

Hudson found the mouth of a great river. He thought this might be the Northwest Passage to the Pacific Ocean. The river was named after him, and is today known as the Hudson River.

Later, Hudson discovered a great bay which is present-day New York Harbor. His voyage led to the beginning of the Dutch fur trade in North America.

Hudson's Last Voyage

In 1610, Hudson left for North America again. This time, he traveled for an English company. He sailed north, around the Orkney Islands and on to Iceland. The sea was cold and foggy, but the crew caught lots of fish.

Hudson landed in Iceland, and found a hot spring for the men to bathe in. They sailed to Greenland, and then on to North America. They were in cold seas, full of mountains of ice, called **icebergs**.

South of Baffin Island, the men entered what is now called Hudson Strait. By now, many of the men were sick, and Hudson thought that it was best to spend the winter in the shelter of James Bay. At first, the men had little to eat. As the weather got warmer, they caught ducks and other sea birds. At last, the ice melted, and the ship was able to sail.

▶ This is an artist's idea of what happened to Henry Hudson. The picture shows him drifting in the icy seas with his son and one of the seven crew members. No one knows what really happened.

The men thought that Hudson had cheated them, and that he had stolen some of the food. There was a mutiny. Hudson, his son, and seven other men were put into a small boat. The rest of the crew returned to England after many battles with the local Inuit people on their return voyage. In England, they were put in prison for the mutiny. Hudson and his men were never seen again. As far as we know, they died in the icy seas.

Hudson had failed to find the Northwest Passage, but his name lives on in some of the places he explored, such as Hudson Bay and the Hudson River.

Voyage to the Southern Land

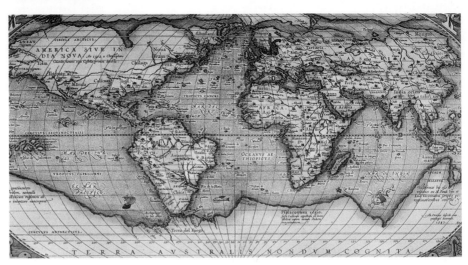

▶ This map dates from 1587. Compare it with the map on page 4. By this time, the mapmakers had a very good idea of the shape of the continents, and where they were. They still did not know about Australia.

When we look at a globe, we can see that there is much more ocean than land in the southern **hemisphere**, or the southern half of the world. Until about 400 years ago, people thought that there must be a continent there as big as Europe and Asia together. Nobody had seen this continent, but it was known as "the unknown southern land."

Today, we know that there are two continents which lie wholly in the southern hemisphere. One is Australia, and the other is the frozen continent of Antarctica.

The South Pacific

The Portuguese had discovered the route to the Spice Islands in 1511. Spain also traded in the South Pacific after Magellan's voyage around the world. They traded mainly with the Philippines. Later, the Dutch drove the Portuguese out of the Spice Islands. The Dutch East India Company became the biggest trader in the South Pacific. The headquarters of their trading company was at Batavia, which is now called Jakarta, Indonesia.

▶ The Portuguese reached the Spice Islands in 1511. At that time, the islands were already famous because of the two spices, cloves and nutmeg, which grew there. These islands, which today are called the Moluccas, lie about halfway between the Philippines and Australia.

The First Sight of Australia

The first people to live in Australia were the **Aborigines**. These people probably crossed to Australia from Asia about 20,000 years ago. Many others may have seen or landed in Australia over the years.

The first person we know about was Willem Jantszoon, a Dutchman. He saw Cape York, in northern Australia, in 1606. Ten years later, another Dutchman named Dirk Hartog landed in western Australia.

Abel Tasman

In 1642, a Dutchman named Abel Tasman sailed from Batavia to find Australia. He sailed across the southern Indian Ocean. He was blown onwards by strong winds from the west called the Roaring Forties. These winds blow around the world across the southern oceans. There is hardly any land to slow them down.

Abel Tasman sailed south of Australia, but he did not see land until he reached a large island which he called "Van Diemen's Island." Later, it was named "Tasmania" after Tasman himself.

Then, Tasman sailed northeast, driven by the northeast winds which usually blow there. He found South Island, New Zealand. Then, he sailed back to Batavia. He had sailed right around Australia, but he had not seen the mainland once!

A French sailor named Louis-Antoine de Bougainville came close to finding the fertile east coast of Australia. He sailed around the world between 1766 and 1769. He saw the Great Barrier Reef off Australia's eastern coast.

On this voyage, de Bougainville found Tahiti. This is a large island in the South Pacific. The island people were very friendly, and de Bougainville thought the island was a paradise.

▲ Louis-Antoine de Bougainville was a French sailor who traveled in the Pacific Ocean. He sailed in a ship called *La Boudeuse*. He was the first person from Europe to reach Tahiti. De Bougainville and his men stayed there for only thirteen days.

The Pacific Explorer

James Cook was born in 1728. He joined the British Navy in 1755, and quickly rose to become the captain of his own ship. He served in Canada where he was in charge of the ship, *Mercury*. There, he showed himself to be a good mapmaker. He learned a lot about the stars and navigation also.

▲ Captain James Cook was born in Yorkshire, England in 1728. He first went to sea in a merchant ship when he was eighteen. Later, he became famous as a great navigator.

A Voyage to the South Seas

In June, 1769, the planet Venus was due to pass between the earth and the sun. The Royal Society in Britain studied such events. Cook had seen a similar **eclipse** of the sun when he was sailing in the North Atlantic. As a result of Cook's knowledge of stars and maps, the Royal Society chose him to be the captain of their ship, which was going to the island of Tahiti in the Pacific Ocean. Venus would be easy to study from there. The Royal Society gave Cook a ship called *Endeavour*. This ship had a crew of ninety-seven men. Among his crew, Cook had people who studied plants. These people were botanists. There was also a person who studied the stars, or an astronomer.

▲ This is a model of the *Endeavour*. The ship was only about a hundred feet long. She had been a coal ship off the coast of northeast England. Cook had sailed ships like her before. She was a very stable, strong ship.

Life on the *Endeavour*

Cook prepared for the voyage with great care. He did not want his crew to get scurvy, so he asked advice about the kind of food to take with him. The *Endeavour* carried lots of orange and lemon juice, salted meat, cabbage, and dried soup. Cook was strict about the crew eating the right food. He showed the men that the officers ate the same as they did. He punished those who did not eat as he ordered.

Cook kept his men busy all day. They cleaned the ship, repaired the sails, and practiced with the ship's guns. Cook took care of his men, but he did not let them disobey him. He knew that a healthy, busy crew would mean success.

Cook in Tahiti

Cook left Britain in August, 1768. He sailed around Cape Horn and on to Tahiti. He ordered his men to behave well with the island people. These people were friendly, but they stole many of Cook's things. He almost lost his measuring instrument, the **quadrant**. Cook needed this to record the movement of Venus.

On June 3, 1769, the **transit** of Venus took place. Cook and his crew stayed in Tahiti until July 13.

▼ Cook carried artists and scientists with him on his journeys to the South Pacific. The artists drew pictures of life there. These are war canoes in Tahiti.

The New Zealand Coast

After leaving Tahiti, Cook and his crew sailed the *Endeavour* southwest across the Pacific. A man from Tahiti named Tupaia sailed with them. On October 7, the east coast of the north island of New Zealand was sighted. Cook landed in a small bay. He was met by the local people called the Maoris. Tupaia talked to them, but fighting broke out.

▲ The Maori people were good farmers and sailors. They were also fine artists. Maoris have always made beautiful carvings. These can still be seen today.

On October 11, Cook left the bay which he named Poverty Bay. He sailed north up the east coast. He met more Maoris who traded with Cook and his men. Cook and the scientists were able to learn a lot about the Maoris. They were good farmers, and they lived in sturdy, well-built houses. Many of the Maoris had colored **tattoos** on their backs, chests, and faces. Later, tattoos became very common among sailors.

Cook sailed around the two main islands of New Zealand. His course was a figure eight. Cook charted the coast and the strait between the two islands. It is now named Cook Strait after him. His maps showed that New Zealand was not part of a southern continent. The maps are so good that sailors can still use them today.

The Great Barrier Reef

Cook left Botany Bay and set sail northwards. By June, they were sailing through **coral** islands. These are part of the Great Barrier Reef. The reef stretches along the east coast of Australia for over 1,250 miles. It is a dangerous place for sailors. The ships can be badly damaged by jagged coral under the surface of the sea. Coral has a hard surface and is made up of tiny sea creatures. Suddenly, the ship hit the coral. The *Endeavour* was stuck there. Cook ordered that anything that was not required be thrown into the sea. The *Endeavour* was dragged off the coral, but there was a huge hole in its side. Cook blocked it up. He stretched two sails across the hole and packed the sails in with dung from the animals on board. It took seven weeks to repair the ship.

▲ Cook's party landed in Botany Bay on the east coast of Australia in April, 1770. Cook called the new land New South Wales.

Botany Bay

On March 31, 1770, the *Endeavour* set a course west across the Tasman Sea. Cook wanted to find Tasmania. Like Tasman, he thought it was part of the mainland of Australia. The wind drove them farther north. On April 9, they sighted a sandy coast with trees and small bushes. It was the east coast of Australia. Cook followed the coast northwards until he reached a large, safe bay to anchor in. He called this Botany Bay, because of the many new plants that the botanists found there. It was in Botany Bay that Cook and his men first saw the Aborigines of Australia.

▲ The Great Barrier Reef stretches for 1,250 miles along the east coast of Australia. Where the sea breaks over the coral, the water is very rough. This reef was a great danger to sailors like Captain Cook.

From the Pacific to the Atlantic

Once the *Endeavour* was repaired, Cook and his crew sailed northward again. They spent eight days making their way through the coral. Then, Cook found a gap in the Great Barrier Reef, and sailed into open sea. This gap is now called Cook's Passage.

After seventeen days, Cook reached the most northern point of Australia. He sailed west through the Torres Strait, and headed along the coast of New Guinea. Cook now saw that New Guinea was not part of Australia. He sailed west towards the Spice Islands, and reached Batavia on October 10, 1770.

By now, many of the men were sick. Cook set sail for Britain and reached there on July 13, 1771. He had sailed 41,875 miles, and made maps of 5,000 miles of unknown coastline. None of his men had died of scurvy.

Cook made a second voyage to the Pacific Ocean between the years 1772 and 1775. He sailed in the Antarctic Ocean and landed on New Zealand. He also mapped many Pacific islands.

▼ The route of Abel Tasman around Australia, and the three voyages of discovery made by Captain Cook.

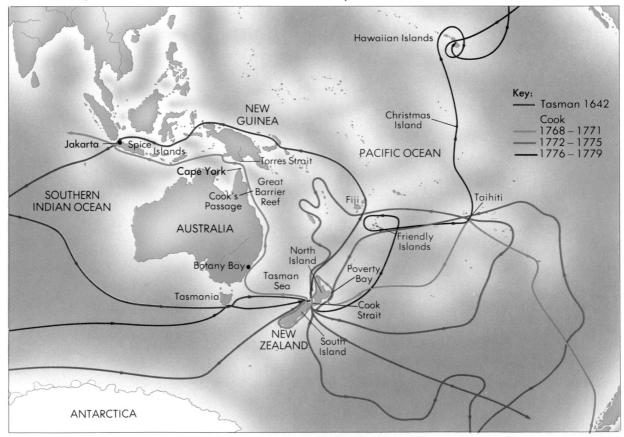

Cook's Last Voyage

In 1776, Cook set out on his third voyage with two ships, the *Resolution* and the *Discovery*. His aim was to find a passage around North America from the Pacific Ocean into the Atlantic Ocean. He sailed around the Cape of Good Hope and eastward by way of Tasmania and New Zealand. The ships sailed on to the Friendly Islands. They arrived there at the end of April, 1777. Cook and his crews rested there until the end of July. Then, they sailed east to Tahiti and north to Christmas Island and the Sandwich Islands. We now call the Sandwich Islands, Hawaii. There, they traded with the islanders.

In February, 1778, Cook sailed across the Pacific Ocean towards North America. He landed at Vancouver Island in Canada, and traded with the people there. Then, Cook set off to explore the coasts of Canada and Alaska and the Bering Strait. He passed through the Strait into the Chuckchi Sea which is north of the Arctic Circle. His men hunted for walrus along the coast. Cook tried to sail west along the north coast of Siberia, but was forced back south by the icy seas.

The Death of Cook

Cook went south to spend the winter in Hawaii. He reached there in late October. His ships were met by 800 canoes. The people thought he was a god. Cook stayed in Hawaii for nearly three months. Then, one night, some islanders stole a boat from the *Discovery*. A fight started and Cook was killed.

Cook had explored more of the world's oceans than anyone before him. His maps and writings helped many explorers who came after him.

▲ Cook's last journey was made with two ships, the *Discovery* and the *Resolution*. These were both small ships, and very much like the *Endeavour*. In this picture, the *Resolution* is making its way through the ice. The *Discovery* is in the distance.

▶ Cook was killed in Hawaii in 1779. A carpenter who traveled with him made a sketch of what happened. His brother, John Clevely, painted this picture later.

33

The *Kon-Tiki*

Many people have sailed the oceans to prove an idea, or **theory**. Thor Heyerdahl is a Norwegian who has spent many years learning about life in the South Pacific. He had new ideas about where the people of the South Pacific came from. He studied the giant statues on Easter Island, and thought they were like the statues made by the Inca people of Peru in South America. The people of Easter Island had a god called Tiki. Heyerdahl thought this might be another name for an Inca god called Viracocha. The Easter Island people had a story, or **legend**, about a leader called Kon-Tiki. They said he had crossed the sea from the east. Heyerdahl thought that the people on Easter Island and the other South Pacific islands had come across the Pacific Ocean from Peru on rafts.

Building the Raft

Heyerdahl wanted to show the world that his theory was right. He built a raft from **balsa** wood logs with a deck made of bamboo. There was a small cabin with a banana leaf roof. There were **mangrove** wood masts and a large square sail. The Incas could have built such a raft with these materials.

On the April 28, 1947, Heyerdahl set sail from Callâo in Peru, and went westward across the Pacific Ocean toward the South Pacific islands. He took with him six friends and a parrot. Heyerdahl took enough food for four months. Some sailors thought the voyage would take over a year. Others thought the balsa logs would soak up water, and the raft would sink.

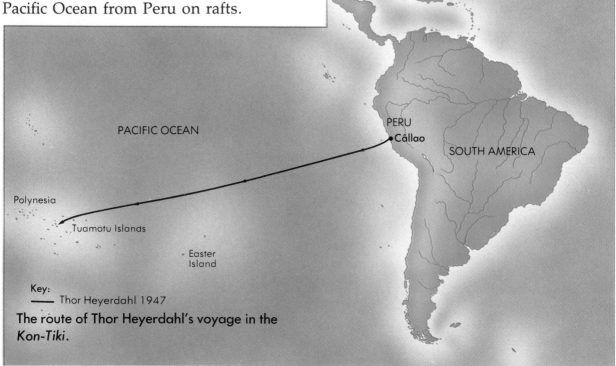

Key:
—— Thor Heyerdahl 1947

The route of Thor Heyerdahl's voyage in the *Kon-Tiki*.

Dangers of the Voyage

As the sea grew calmer, sharks began to appear. At first, the men were afraid. They thought the sharks would smash the raft. It became clear, however, that the sharks were not interested in them and would not attack.

One day, a sleeping bag fell off the raft. One of the men, Hermann, tried to catch it, and fell in the water. The raft was moving fast. Soon, he was left behind. One of the other men attached a lifebelt to a line. Then, he dived in and swam to his friend. They both held onto the lifebelt, and were pulled back to safety.

▲ Thor Heyerdahl's raft, the *Kon-Tiki*, is now in a museum in Norway. Heyerdahl sailed 5,000 miles in the *Kon-Tiki* from Peru to Polynesia.

Across the Pacific

There is a strong current running west across the Pacific Ocean. This is called the Humboldt Current. This carried the raft westward. The seas grew rougher, and huge waves broke over the raft. Heyerdahl and his friends found that the water ran off the raft easily.

On the raft, there was a giant steering oar. It got harder and harder to control the oar as the waves got stronger. It took two men to hold it. They took turns controlling the oar for an hour at a time during the day and night. At last, the wind died down, and the men were able to steer the raft more easily.

▲ The *Kon-Tiki* crossing the Pacific in 1947.

In Sight of Land

In July, the men on the *Kon-Tiki* began to see frigate birds. Frigate birds are a sign that land is near. More and more birds were seen. Heyerdahl set course to follow them. Then, they saw a warm **haze** ahead. This was air rising from hot sand. On July 30, they saw an island, but they could not steer toward it because the current was too strong. Four days later, they saw another island ahead. They were very happy.

▼ Thor Heyerdahl and one of his crew on the *Kon-Tiki*. Heyerdahl proved that this kind of raft could travel for very long distances.

Failure to Land

The men were not happy for long. Between them and the land, there was a coral reef. Between the reef and the shore, the sea was very rough and churning like boiling water. The raft got as close to the island as it could. The men could see huts and people on the island. There was no way they could get through the reef. Then, they saw two men in a canoe rowing toward them. The canoe had come through a hidden gap in the reef. Heyerdahl spoke to the men in the canoe. Soon, other canoes followed, and they tried to pull the raft through the gap. The wind was against them. In the end, the people in the canoes gave up.

The raft drifted on for three days. The men had been at sea now for a hundred days. Then, to their horror, they found that the raft was drifting straight for a reef. They did all they could to save it. They could not risk being cut to pieces on the reef after they had come so far.

The End of the *Kon-Tiki*

The *Kon-Tiki* was lifted into the air by the sea. Then, the raft crashed down onto the reef. Somehow, it stayed in one piece. The men were shaken, but they were alive. The raft was stuck on the reef. The men swam for the shore beyond it. They were safe at last on the sandy beach with its palm trees. Heyerdahl and his men had made it to the Tuamotu Islands, in the South Pacific.

Since Heyerdahl's journey, many experts have said that he may have been wrong about his theory. He did, however, prove the journey was possible.

▼ *Ra* was made in Egypt close to the pyramids. It was made by using papyrus reeds. Boats built in ancient Egypt thousands of years ago were also built of papyrus. Students helped to pull the *Ra* overland to the place where it was launched.

Further Journeys

Heyerdahl went on to make further journeys in simple boats across seas and oceans. He wanted to show how it was possible for people in the past to move from place to place. In 1970, he made a voyage in a boat made of water plants, called **reeds**. The boat was called the *Ra*. This was a copy of an Egyptian reed boat. He crossed the Atlantic Ocean from Morocco in North Africa to Barbados in the West Indies. He wanted to show that the people of Egypt could have reached America a few thousand years ago.

▲ Thor Heyerdahl with his boat, the *Ra*. Heyerdahl proved that people from ancient Egypt could have traveled across the Atlantic Ocean.

Exploring Under the Ocean

Under the sea lies a whole new world. There are ridges, valleys, and mountains. There are vast numbers of brightly colored fish. Some fish live on the sea bed, and never come to the surface. Under the sea, there are also plants and creatures never seen near the surface. This world lies hidden from human eyes. The first serious attempt to map the ocean floor was made in 1873 by the crew of the British Navy ship, the *Challenger*. Many scientists sailed on this ship to study the Atlantic, the Pacific, and Indian Oceans. The depth and shape, or formation, of the ocean floor was measured. Temperatures were recorded. Also, the scientists collected many types of plants. However, it was not until 1926 that people were able to see the ocean floor for themselves.

People under the Sea

A **diving chamber** is a small metal container with small, round windows, or **portholes**. In this chamber, people are lowered into the ocean. Air is brought into the chamber through airlines from the surface. The first of these chambers to descend into very deep water was the American **bathysphere**. In 1934, it descended over 2,500 feet into the Atlantic Ocean.

In 1953, a new diving chamber was invented. Auguste Piccard was a Swiss scientist. He designed what he called a **bathyscaphe**. The bathyscaphe had to withstand the immense **pressure** of the ocean water against its walls. It had steel walls which were three and a half inches thick. The vessel had special plastic portholes. These were six inches thick. There were chambers which filled with water. These forced the vessel downward. In an early test, Piccard descended to over 9,750 feet.

In 1960, Jacques Piccard, Auguste's son, took a new bathyscaphe called *Trieste* to the Mariana Trench in the Pacific Ocean. This is 36,000 feet deep, the deepest part of the ocean. It took five hours to reach the bottom. The crew stayed on the ocean floor under 200,000 tons of water for twenty minutes. Then, they surfaced again.

◀ The *Challenger* was a warship once. She was converted, so that she could be used for scientific work. Between 1872 and 1876, the *Challenger* sailed more than 70,000 miles. Scientists on board discovered many species of sea creatures that no one had known about before.

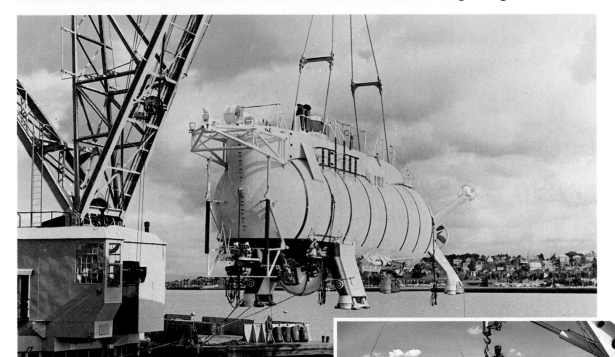

▲ This is Jacques Piccard's bathyscaphe, the *Trieste*. Underneath it are the cameras and lights the scientists used when they were deep under the water.

▲ Jacques Cousteau made many television programs about life under the sea. Here, he is on his boat, the *Calypso*.

Living Underwater

People have to breathe underwater. The early divers had air lines to the surface. In 1942, Jacques Cousteau invented the **aqualung**. This has tanks of **oxygen** which the diver can carry on his back. A tube from the tanks to the diver's mouth allows him to breathe. The aqualung provides the diver with much more freedom underwater. Cousteau and his team reached depths of 225/300 feet. The aqualung is now used by divers when they are searching in the oceans for oil and precious metals.

In 1949, Cousteau bought the vessel, the *Calypso*. He used this as a center, or **base**, from which to make underwater TV programs. Later in 1962, Cousteau built the *Conshelf*. This is a complete home beneath the sea. People spent a week working in the *Conshelf* at a depth of thirty-five feet under the Mediterranean Sea. A year later, five men lived under the Red Sea in a *Conshelf* for a month.

New Challenges

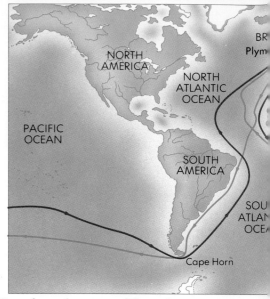

In this century, a new kind of sailor has appeared. These sailors want to be the first to make certain kinds of ocean crossings or to break world records. They sail alone in small vessels. It is one person against the wind and the sea. This needs a special kind of courage and great willpower.

Around the World in *Gipsy Moth*

Francis Chichester was an airplane pilot when he was a young man. He made flights alone, or **solo**, across the oceans and seas of the world. In 1931, Chichester was the first person to fly alone from mainland Australia to Tasmania across the Tasman Sea. Later that year, he made the first solo flight northwards across the Pacific Ocean from New Zealand to Japan.

In 1960, when he was fifty-nine years old, Chichester became famous as a sailor. He took part in the first **transatlantic** race for solo sailors. He crossed the Atlantic Ocean in just over forty days, and won the race.

In 1966, Chichester set out from Plymouth, England, in a boat called *Gipsy Moth IV*. It was only fifty-three feet long. His aim was to sail around the world with only one stop. This was to be at Sydney, Australia. It is very tiring for one person to handle a boat alone for such a long journey. Chichester managed well, even though he was not young. He was almost killed a number of times. Often, the seas were so rough that he could not sleep for days. Chichester circled the world in 190 days. He returned to Plymouth to a hero's welcome.

◀ Francis Chichester's boat, *Gipsy Moth IV*, leaving Sydney, Australia. Although the boat was small, it was still very hard work for one person to handle.

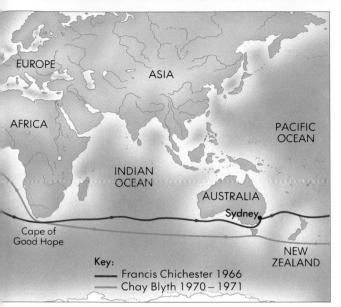

▲ The solo voyages of Francis Chichester and Chay Blyth around the world.

Chay Blyth

Chay Blyth was a Scottish soldier. In 1966, he and another soldier, John Ridgeway, challenged two men to a rowing race. This race was across the Atlantic Ocean. Blyth and Ridgeway's boat was an old fishing vessel. It cost them $370.00 to build. The other two men had a special boat built for the race which cost them $4,000.

In June, 1966, Blyth and Ridgeway began the race from Cape Cod, Massachusetts. They had 3,500 miles of sea to cross to Ireland. The idea was to test themselves to the very limit.

It took them ninety-two days to reach Ireland. The other two men were not so lucky. Their boat was found upside down in the middle of the ocean. The men themselves were never found.

In 1970, Blyth set out alone from Britain in a fifty-eight foot, steel sailing boat called *British Steel*. He wanted to circle the world traveling west. This is a route which means sailing against the wind. His course was to sail to Cape Horn, and then continue westward through the South Pacific. There was no land to break the force of the powerful wind. He was sailing against the Roaring Forties. One sailor said of Blyth that he must have felt he was trying to ride a bike up a mountain. In 292 days, he made one of the greatest solo voyages of all time.

In 1973, Blyth entered the first Around the World sailing race. He and his crew made the 26,875-mile voyage from Portsmouth, England and back in a record time of 144 days.

▲ Chay Blyth's yacht was named *British Steel*. Chay Blyth made a very difficult journey when he sailed westward around the world. This was much harder than traveling eastward, because the winds were always against him.

Women Sailors

Until recently, few women chose a career at sea. However, a number of women sailors have recently become famous because of their record-breaking sea journeys.

Naomi James

Naomi James was born on a farm in New Zealand. In 1971, she came to Britain by ship. Later, she married Rob James. He was a sailor and a friend of Chay Blyth.

From 1977 to 1978, Naomi James used Chay Blyth's boat, the *Empress Crusader*, for a record-breaking voyage. In 1977, Naomi set out from Britain to sail around the world alone. She was seasick from the start. In the Indian Ocean, the storms almost smashed the vessel.

Naomi managed to keep on course and carry out repairs to the ship. In the Pacific Ocean, far from land, the vessel turned right over and then righted itself. Waves over thirty feet high threw the vessel forward. Yet, some weeks later, Naomi sailed past stormy Cape Horn with no trouble and sailed on to the Falkland Islands. From there, she made good speed and nine months after the *Empress Crusader* set out, Naomi was back in Britain. She was the first woman to sail solo around the world.

Clare Francis

Clare Francis was a dancer and a model. In 1973, she sailed across the Atlantic Ocean alone. The next year, she took part in the Round Britain Race and came in third.

▲ Naomi James sailed alone in the yacht, *Empress Crusader*. She made the trip around the world from 1977 to 1978. Here, she is checking her position by the sun.

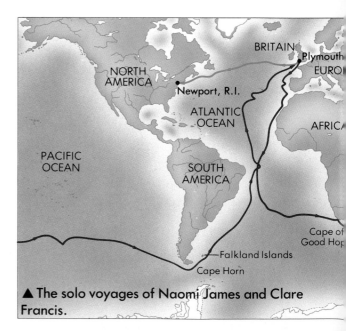

▲ The solo voyages of Naomi James and Clare Francis.

Two years later, Clare wanted to enter the Transatlantic Race. There were 200 entrants in the race. Four were women. Clare's boat was only thirty-nine feet long.

The race took her through very bad weather. Waves thirty feet high swept over the boat. She sailed through deep fogs and passed huge icebergs.

Near the end of the journey, her **self-steering gear**, which guides the boat, was damaged. Clare had to lift it onto the boat. It weighed forty pounds more than she did. Clare spent five hours trying to repair it. At last, she found a way to rope the self-steering gear onto the boat. Twenty-nine days after leaving Britain, Clare was the first woman to reach Newport, Rhode Island. Only one other woman completed the race.

▲ Between 1977 and 1978, Clare Francis raced around the world in this yacht, the *ADC Accutrac*. She had a crew of eleven people with her. Clare and her crew came in fifth in the race.

The Oceans Today

Hundreds of years ago, people set out in small sailing ships to explore unknown seas. They were looking for new trading routes and other lands. They made maps of the oceans and the coasts they discovered. Often, their voyages were dangerous and many sailors lost their lives. Today, ships are much bigger and have more powerful engines. They have computers to help sailors to find their way. In spite of this, the oceans can still be dangerous.

The oceans take up nearly three quarters of the surface of the earth. We do not yet know everything about the ocean depths. People continue to search for oil and minerals which might lie under the ocean floor. In many ways, ocean exploration continues.

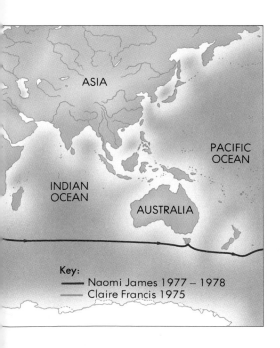

ASIA

PACIFIC OCEAN

INDIAN OCEAN

AUSTRALIA

Key:
—— Naomi James 1977 – 1978
—— Claire Francis 1975

Quiz

How much can you remember about this book? Try this quiz. Use the glossary and index to help you find your answers.

1. Here are some names of famous ocean travelers with the letters scrambled. Unscramble them to find the correct names.

   a) SCOUMBUL, b) NAGELLAM,
   c) RAKED, d) OCKO, e) SHUDON,
   f) TUSCEAUO, g) REDHEALHY

2. Can you guess what this sentence says?

   Captain James _____ said he _____ to go "not only _____ than anyone _____ before, but as _____ as it was _____ for _____ to go."

   Clue: This man made three great journeys. He was killed in Hawaii.

3. Put the following events in the order they took place.

   a) Cousteau builds the *Conshelf*.
   b) Magellan sets out to sail around the world.
   c) The first solo sea journey around the world is made by a woman.
   d) Frobisher sails in the Arctic Ocean.
   e) Cook sees Australia for the first time.

4. Match the descriptions given in (a) to (e) with the words numbered (1) to (5) below them.

   a) The island that Columbus thought was Japan
   b) An island in the Pacific visited by Captain Cook
   c) A famous raft which was sailed across the Pacific Ocean
   d) A vehicle used for deep-sea exploration
   e) A small boat used for a solo voyage around the world

   1) *Trieste*
   2) Cuba
   3) *Kon-Tiki*
   4) *Gipsy Moth IV*
   5) Tahiti

5. Complete the following sentences with a), b), c) or d):

   1) Goods carried on board ships are called the
      a) sails.
      b) cargo.
      c) holds.
      d) helms.

   2) Columbus's own ship was called the
      a) *Vittoria*.
      b) *Santa María*.
      c) *Golden Hind*.
      d) *Endeavour*.

   3) One of the early sailors to reach North America was
      a) Marco Polo.
      b) Vasco da Gama.
      c) Prince Henry the Navigator.
      d) John Cabot.

4) The first ship to sail around the world was the
a) *Golden Hind*.
b) *Concepción*.
c) *Vittoria*.
d) *Trinidad*.

5) Magellan was killed on the island of
a) Tahiti.
b) Cuba.
c) Cebu.
d) Hawaii.

6) The *Conshelf* is
a) a storage place on board ship.
b) an underwater reef.
c) a large fish.
d) a home under the sea.

6. How many ocean travelers can you find with names beginning with C, H and P?

7. Which ocean would you be in if you
a) were in an area full of seaweed called the Sargossa Sea?
b) had the monsoon winds against you?

c) found yourself off Baffin Island?
d) were sailing past Easter Island?
e) were near the South Pole?

8. Who or what
a) crossed the Atlantic Ocean in a reed boat called the *Ra*?
b) first reached North America with long boats?
c) sent captains in caravels to explore the West Coast of Africa?
d) is a record of the voyage made by a ship?
e) is a strong flow of water in an ocean?

9. Are these statements True or False?
a) An aqualung is a deep-sea diving vessel.
b) Columbus was the first sailor from Europe to reach North America.
c) When Drake started on his voyage around the world his crew thought they were going to Egypt.
d) There are three continents which lie wholly in the southern hemisphere.
e) There is an island called Christmas.

Answers

1. a) COLUMBUS, b) MAGELLAN, c) DRAKE, d) COOK, e) HUDSON, f) COUSTEAU, g) HEYERDAHL.

2. Captain James Cook said that he wanted to go, "not only farther than anyone had been before, but as far as it was possible for man to go."

3. (b), (d), (e), (d), (a), (c)

4. (a) 2, (b) 5, (c) 3, (d) 1, (e) 4

5. 1 (b), 2 (b), 3 (d), 4 (c), 5 (c), 6 (d)

6. Cook, Columbus, Cão, Cabots, Cousteau, Chichester, Hanno, Hudson, Hartog, Heyerdahl, Prince Henry the Navigator, Pytheas, Pinzóns, Piccards

7. (a) Atlantic, (b) Indian, (c) Arctic, (d) Pacific, (e) Antarctic

8. (a) Thor Heyerdahl, (b) Leif Ericsson, (c) Prince Henry the Navigator, (d) logbook, (e) current

9. (a) False, (b) False, (c) True, (d) False,

Glossary

Aborigines: the name given to the first people to live in Australia. It comes from the Latin word meaning "from the beginning."

anchor: to lower a steel structure into the water to hold a ship in one place.

aqualung: a breathing apparatus which divers carry on their backs. This consists of a cylinder of compressed air which is attached by a pipe to a face mask.

balsa: a South American tree with a very soft, light wood.

base: a place from which an organization or expedition works. It will keep its main supplies at the base.

bathyscaphe: a deep-sea diving vessel with an observation capsule which can reach ocean depths of over 32,000 feet.

bathysphere: a round, strong deep-sea diving vessel made of steel which is lowered to the seabed by a cable.

bay: part of the coast where the land curves inward. This sometimes forms a natural harbor.

caravel: a light, fast ship with two square sails and one triangular sail at the stern.

cargo: a load of goods carried by a ship or plane.

chart: to make a detailed plan or map.

coast: the edge of land next to the sea.

continent: a large mass of land, sometimes including many countries. The earth is divided into seven continents.

convict: a person who is put in prison for committing a crime.

coral: a small sea animal which builds a hard tube of chalk around itself.

course: a direction to follow.

crew: the group of people who work together on a ship or plane.

current: the flow of water within a sea, lake, or river.

diving chamber: a metal vessel which is lowered by cable into the sea. This vessel is supplied with compressed air from above and has portholes so people can see under the sea.

East: the countries of Asia. Asia was often called the East because travelers from Europe journeyed eastwards to get there.

eclipse: the shadow caused by one object blocking off the light of another. During an eclipse of the sun, the moon comes between the sun and the earth.

expedition: an organized journey which is made for a special purpose. Explorers went on expeditions to find out about new lands.

haze: a thin mist.

helm: a device by which a boat is steered.

hemisphere: a half of a sphere. The earth is divided into two hemispheres by the equator.

hold: the part of a ship or plane where goods and baggage are carried.

iceberg: a large piece of ice which floats like an island in the sea. Most of the ice is under the surface of the sea.

legend: an old story about something that is supposed to have happened in the past.

logbook: a book where details of a ship's voyage are kept, particularly movement or events.

mangrove: a tree that grows in shallow coastal water in hot parts of the world.

mast: the long upright pole on a ship which supports the sails.

merchant: a person who buys and sells goods, often dealing with other countries.

metal: any of several substances obtained from under the ground. Iron and gold are metals.

monsoon: a strong wind that changes direction according to the season.

musket: a long barrelled shoulder gun used in the 1600's and 1700's by soldiers.

mutiny to refuse to obey the people in charge. Soldiers and sailors mutiny when they refuse to fight or sail any farther.

navigate: to plan and direct the course of a ship or plane.

oxygen: a gas found in air and water. Oxygen is very important to all plants and animals. We cannot breathe without oxygen.

pearl: a small, white, valuable, stone-like ball found in some oysters and used in jewelry.

pilot: a captain who takes charge of a ship while it is entering or leaving a harbor.

porthole: a type of window built into a ship or plane.

pressure: the action of one thing pressing on or against something else.

quadrant: an instrument used to measure the height of the stars. Sailors used a quadrant to steer their ships in the right direction.

reed: a stalk of a tall, thin, grass-like plant found by the water or in water.

region: a district or area.

route: the way to get from one place to another. Routes are shown on maps and plans.

scurvy: a disease caused by the lack of vitamin C. This vitamin can be found in fresh fruit and vegetables. The disease leads to bleeding of the gums, and damage to the teeth and bones of the body.

self-steering gear: a mechanism used to steer a ship or plane automatically.

solo: describes anything special done by one person.

stable: describes something which is steady in balance or position.

strait: a narrow piece of sea between two larger seas or oceans.

tattoo: to make patterns on the skin with needles and dyes.

theory: a set of ideas or opinion based on reason to explain certain facts.

trader: someone who does business by buying and selling goods.

transatlantic: describes crossing the Atlantic Ocean.

transit: the passage of one heavenly body across the face of another.

voyage: a journey, especially a long one by sea, or air, or in space.

wreck: to ruin or destroy. Ships can be wrecked by storms or rocks.

Index